Break Ups

A Guide to Dealing With Breakups

Table of Contents

Introduction

Heart breaks are painful.
reason of the breakup, it hurts when a significant relationship comes to an end. The feeling of rejection can jumble up a person's emotions, leading him to feel totally unworthy. A person invests emotionally in a romantic relationship or marriage, but not all things are meant to be. Sometimes, due to unprecedented reasons, a relationship has to end. This might leave the person morose and bitter.

But, no matter how deeply rooted the pain is, there is always a way to heal and get better. What is important at such a time is to know the right way to heal and to move on in life. In the very beginning the person should only focus on getting over the ex lover and getting back to his or her normal life. The denial to accept the breakup can be very harmful as it will lead us nowhere and make our life even more complicated. It is important to sort one's life and feelings after a break up.

There are a series of steps that a person can religiously follow to get over the first few days of the breakup, which are very difficult. It is imperative to learn the right way to cope with the separation. Separation is bound to bring with it a dangerous feeling of diffidence and unworthiness. Accept the pain and the oscillating emotions, but resolve to work towards a better you. This book talks about the different steps that will help you achieve this goal. The steps discussed to get through the initial phase of separation will ensure that you don't immerse yourself in a never ending circle of pain and tears. After the initial phase is over, the person is out of the grieving period of breakup. But, then comes the phase where he needs to gather all his strength and move on from his previous life.

This, again, can seem to be an uphill task, but with the steps discussed in this book, a person can look forward to move on in a successful way. Be kind to yourself and love yourself.

Once you learn to do that, rest all will only be a cakewalk.

Chapter 1: Steps to Cope with the Separation

A relationship ends because something is not right in the relationship. But, then why does it hurt so much even when the reason to end a relationship is to make things right? This is because a breakup represents the end of something that could have been. It represents the end of dreams that once two people had shared together. Any romantic association begins on a very high note. A person is high on happiness, excitement and hope. When this excitement and happiness takes an ugly and sour turn, it does pain a lot. Even if the break up happens in a not so ugly way, it is nevertheless painful and morose.

It is difficult to feel empowered or strong right after the break up because at that time the emotions are also jumbled up. It is impossible to jump from the deep oceans of sorrow to the high peaks of happiness. It is more important to take one step at a time. One step taken at the right time in the right direction will help a person pull himself out of the shackles of sorrow. The initial phase includes the days that immediately follow the breakup. Following are few steps that you can follow to get through the initial phase of the breakup:

1. **Take a break from your routine** - Breakups are exhausting. Know that your state will not transform in an hour or in a day. You have to give yourself that time. Therefore, allow yourself to take a break from your normal life. This break will help you to get back on track and also benefit you in the long run. But, use your logical judgment when deciding on the things you want a break from. You might be able to take a break from your dance class, but your boss might not grant you a leave in the middle of an important project.

   Make sure that your life is not getting affected in the wrong way by this break.

If a complete break from the routine is not possible, try to plan your day in a less stressful way. Talk to your friends and make them understand if you wish to cancel on the impending plans. Do not force yourself to go out and have fun at this time. They are your friends, so they will understand. Your current focus should be to get back on track. Do whatever is required for that.

2. **Let the pain out** - Give the pain some channel, and let it all out, be it in form of anger or tears. Each one has a different way of getting over pain. While some might cry into their pillow for the entire night, others might yell and scream at the top of their voice. Do not stop yourself from crying, and do not criticize yourself from being too emotional. It is okay. Scream if you want to; cry out loudly if you want to. Your body will eventually get tired with these extreme emotions. But, before that let your body

and mind cleanse themselves of all that is within. Before you can let go of all the extreme emotions, you have to face them and go through them.

Crying is a form of therapy for it releases all the pent up emotions in the form of tears. You can't force yourself to cry, but if you feel like crying don't stop yourself. You might get an impulse to hit things or break things, but try not to indulge in such pleasures. Though breaking a flower vase or hitting the pillow might not hurt anyone, but doctors suggest avoiding the route of even the smallest form of violence for your healing. Today you might hit a pillow, but tomorrow you might want to hit something bigger. So, it is better to refrain from such activities. Instead, scream as much as you can in your room.

3. **Express yourself through creative channels** - Art and music can be the

best healers and go a long way to uplift the emotional state. Listen to a song that you like or that comforts you in some way. Music can reach the deepest corners of your heart and trigger points that are otherwise unknown to you. Listening to music will help you to release your tension and stress. Don't listen to anything that you don't enjoy or something that is too heavy for you. Listen to something that makes you feel good about yourself or life in general. You can also try your hand at writing.

It is a well known fact that writing is a great stress buster. You don't have to be the greatest writer in the world, or you don't have to write big and fancy words. All that you need to do is to release your pressures through the medium of writing. Write about how you feel, or write a poem. Try your hand at doodling and drawing. Just take the pen and let it sway. Draw about how you feel, or draw random circles and lines. Do whatever you like. Such creative experiences are bound to help you feel better.

4. **Exercise -** It is highly recommended to vent out your emotions through a physical activity of your choice. Though it might be difficult to start a rigorous exercise routine at this stage, a simple enjoyable physical activity that helps you to sweat out would be helpful. Go for a walk if you feel like. The green grass of the park, pleasant wind, chirping birds and company of unknown people can do wonders to a person's psychic. If you don't feel like going out, then do some simple stretches at home. Anything that flexes your muscles and gives your mind another agenda apart from the breakup is good enough. If nothing else, you should aim at doing some easy and light breathing exercises. Breathing exercises help the senses to calm down, leaving the person peaceful.

5. **Know that you are not alone** - Psychologists around the world have reported that approximately 98 percent of people have experienced a heart break, in terms of unrequited love from a crush or a bad breakup with a lover. It might help to know that you are not alone and that people around the world have gone through and survived such phases. Though, such a justification might not lessen the pain, but it might help to see things in perspective. If others can survive a heart break, even you can. Just don't give up and keep at it. A heart break is sad but not the end of the world. There is more to life than the fact that you have had a breakup. A cut on your finger does not mean that your life will end. It only means that you have to take special care of your finger for sometime. Similarly, you need to give yourself some special love and care

because you deserve it more than anybody else.

6. **Break the ties** - Accept that you are bound to be vulnerable immediately after the breakup. Allow yourself some time and do not take hasty decisions. Try to stay away from your ex lover. Breaking these ties will be helpful for you. Irrespective of who broke up, avoid being in contact with your ex. There could be some legal and practical issues that might force you to meet him, such as legal papers or property related stuff. But, otherwise stay away even if you feel you can stay friends. Even if the ex lover suggests that you guys should be in touch, do not do so. This is not the right time to take such a decision. You need to maintain a distance from your ex to get things right in your head.

7. **Take care of yourself** - Take care of the simple but important things of

everyday life. Eat your food on time. Excuse yourself a few times and eat whatever and how much ever you want to, but on the whole maintain a balanced diet. Eat fresh fruits along with right mix of carbohydrates, proteins, vitamins and fiber. This step might not seem very important to someone who is going through an emotional turmoil, but it is very important. The right kind of food helps to keep the brain and body function right. You don't want an upset stomach or pounding headache along with the emotional pain you are going through. Drink water regularly, even if you don't feel like. And, try to sleep for 8 hours every day. When you take care of your body, your body will also respond in the right way, and this step will go a long way in restoring balance back in your life.

Chapter 2: Working Through the Emotional Pain

Life comes to a standstill after a breakup. The world seems dull and lifeless. It is difficult to deal with a broken heart. Everybody likes to believe that the love would be forever, but sometimes as the relationship progresses, you see things that were not visible in the beginning. Nobody foresees a breakup at the beginning of a relationship. There is no cure for pain, but to endure it and bear it. The sooner you do it, the better. You can't postpone your feelings for another day. If you don't feel fine, you don't. Facing your emotions and dealing with them is the only way out. The following steps will guide you when going through an emotional turmoil:

1. **Accept the pain** - Unless and until a person accepts the existence of a wound, it is difficult to heal it. It is important that you acknowledge that it will pain. It is normal to feel sullen, angry and exhausted. You have the right to feel all

these extreme emotions. Even if the romantic relationship was troublesome, ending it is not an easy task. It is always difficult to venture out into the unknown and the unseen. The nervousness and anxiety of the future can be really troublesome.

Give yourself the freedom to go through these pent up emotions. The intensity of these feelings will reduce with the passage of time. But, right now your main focus should be to let yourself be. It is more dangerous to be in a denial mode by pretending to be happy. If you are not happy, you're no. Accept it and face it. Tell yourself that it is fine not to feel fine and happy, and it is fine to be messed up in the head.

2. **Maintain a journal** - You can also keep a daily journal to keep track of your mood swings. Such a journal will help you understand what your progress has

been so far. Take out some time each day, sit and write about how you feel and what you've been up to. If you enjoy writing, you could maintain a nice descriptive journal. But, if you like keeping things short, then just write in brief points. These points should be able to convey your state of mind and general mood for the day. This journal is a book of your progress, so be as honest as possible. If you don't feel too great, there is no need to bluff happiness. The idea of writing everyday is to track your mood swings, so that you can understand your progress and decide how you want to progress in the future.

3. **Start a new hobby or re start an old one** - You can also consider on re starting a hobby that you enjoyed earlier. It could be a very simple activity, but it will go a long way to heal your heart and divert your mind. You can also start a new hobby. There is no harm in

trying out new activities and continuing with the ones you enjoy.

4. **Anger management** - Anger and frustration is a part of the process of moving on. You are bound to feel angry over things you can't set right. But, this anger would only bring you down if you don't learn how to channelize it. Learn techniques to release your anger effectively and positively. Dance your heart away if you enjoy dancing. Meditate if you enjoy that. If nothing else, just sit quietly and focus on your breathing. Count your breaths, while resolving to release your anger. Breathe in peace and happiness and breathe out anger and frustration. Practice this technique regularly to calm down your mind and release tension from your muscles.

5. **Talk to someone** - If nothing seems to help you then you should consider

talking to somebody who would lend you a shoulder to cry on. Your loved ones worry for your well being, and they would be more than happy to help you. Talk to a friend or a relative, and tell them about all that you are going through. They will definitely understand you. If you don't want to talk to anyone you know, you can also consider consulting a psychologist. You should consider doing this if you are unable to help yourself, no matter how much efforts you put in. A psychologist will understand your condition and will show you the right way ahead. You can share your feelings without any fear with your doctor. Also, the psychologist is an expert in such cases, so he would be able to suggest the right things to do in this case.

Chapter 3: Things not to do

It could be just a case of unrequited love or a painful separation from a loved one, break ups are never easy. They bring with them the feeling of rejection, loneliness and dejection. A person dealing with a heart break isolates himself from the world, only to grieve in pain for the lost love. He feels all alone and finds no solace in the world around him. Such people can become very vulnerable and can engulf themselves with extreme negativity and sadness. Though some amount of sadness is important to get over the ex lover, but too much of anything can be harmful. While going through a breakup, there are a few things that you should refrain from, no matter how high the impulse to do them is.

1. **Avoid posting any details on the social media** - Social media is as much a culprit as a boon. While it can help you to stay connected and learn more about the world while sitting in the comfort of

your home, it can also fill you in with some unnecessary details. Pledge to stay away from the social media for a few days. The world would not stop if you don't post the details of your personal life on the internet.

Do not share your feelings or anything related to the breakup on the internet. And, do not go out of the way to post pictures or text that show that you are happy and unaffected by the breakup. Just take a break from all your social media accounts. Also, make it a point to not check your ex lover's accounts. Checking his account will throw into the middle of that unwanted circle of pain and grief. And, you definitely don't want that.

2. **Stay away from unhealthy ways** - Drinking and smoking might seem like great options, but they are not good for the person in the long run. There is

nothing you will gain by smoking and drinking. Don't indulge in unhealthy means to feel better. No matter what, never drink alone. This can be hazardous because you would not know when to stop, what to do and what not.

3. **Avoid negative thoughts and talks** - There are all kinds of people in this world. Some can crush you in a second; while others can help you uplift your soul. You should decide wisely on the kind of interactions you want to have with the people around you. By all means, avoid negative people. Avoid such a person who can make you feel low about yourself or about something that has happened to you. Such a person can successfully implant negative thoughts in your brain without your own knowledge.

    These negative thoughts will hamper your progress. Instead, talk to positive people who see positive in everything that happens. Such people will help you to realize that what has happened is not the biggest disaster and that you are worth better things in life. Also, avoid anything that doesn't make you feel good about yourself. Avoid sad and gloomy TV shows. These shows will trigger your negative and sad emotions, making you miserable. Watch shows that help you to divert your attention to other things and topics.

4. **Do not contact your ex lover –** There could be times when you get the impulse to contact your ex lover for reconciliation or to yell at him for what he did. Whatever is the case, do not call or text him. Either block him or delete his number. This step is necessary because at such a time you might say things that you will repent on later. Maintain no contact with your ex lover.

Chapter 4: Steps to Stay Strong and Move On

After you've successfully gotten over the initial stage of controlling your emotional swings, you have the uphill task of getting back with your life. A breakup should not disrupt your life so much that you lose track of your own life. It might seem daunting, but just as you could glide through the initial phase, this moving on phase will also be achievable once you decide to do it. Following are a few steps that can guide you:

1. **Accept that the relationship is over** - Accept that the relationship is over for good. Remembering your ex lover or the time spent with him or her will only digress you from your path to recovery. It is imperative that you realize that what is gone is gone for good. You should stop hoping for any way to reconcile with your lover. This is the time to hope for a good future by accepting the truth and moving on.

Deciding to remain good friends with the ex lover might also not be a great idea at this stage because this is the time to focus on self and personal growth. This is time for renewal, which is not possible unless the past is buried.

Even if there is the slightest chance of maintaining a healthy friendship with the ex lover, this time is not right for it because the wounds have only begun to heal, and a step like this might harm you and leave you to at a point where you had begun. This is definitely not what you want. So, just focus on the self and forget about renewing any ties with the ex lover.

2. **Stay strong** - Amidst all the ups and downs, you have to stay strong. There will be days when you get up and feel that you have figured this out and have healed yourself. And, there would be days when you feel that nothing is fine

and you will never be able to get over this pain. It is important that you maintain a sense of realism.

You have to know that there will be good and bad days, but what should remain constant is your will to get over and move on. Even when you don't feel right, do not give too much importance to your emotional state and keep repeating to yourself that this phase is temporary and will go away. By now, you should be able slowly get back to your routine life. Focus on the agenda of the day.

3. **Introspection and reflection** - It always helps to reflect and introspect. You might choose the medium of your choice. While some would just sit and ponder on the situation, others might want to write down about their realizations. Sit calmly and think about the reasons of the breakup. Knowing these reasons will help you to not commit the same mistakes in the future.

Make clear notes of why you think things went wrong. It could be your mistake or the other person's mistake, just be honest with yourself.

Once you know the reasons, also think about what you could have done better in the situation. If it is difficult to go through the entire experience at one time, so take out some time every day and sit and write about your emotional state. Break the entire experience into different parts and go through them individually each day. The entire process might seem very technical, but remember that your aim right now should be to learn and move on. This introspection is not to feel bad about yourself or the breakup. It is only a way of learning something from the entire experience, so that this experience can be applied in future engagements.

4. **Learn from the experience** - Regardless of how good or bad an association is there is always a hidden learning. If you wish to learn, you can learn from anything and everything. After you have settled down a bit, it is important that you analyze the entire situation and learn from it. What was your mistake? What could you've done better? What would you do better if faced by a similar situation in your next relationship? Have you matured as a person? Think about such questions, without getting too emotional. Keep a logical head and be true to yourself. This is to make sure you never repeat a mistake. Doing this will not only help you to grow as a person, but would also help you in your next relationship.

5. **Enjoy the little things** – Real happiness is not in the biggest of things, but in the small pleasures. Involve yourself in simple pleasures of life, such

as gardening and painting. Go for walks. Say a hello to a stranger. Help someone who needs to your help. Reorganize your closet and clean your room. Bake a cake. Give away things that you don't need any more. These small things might seem unimportant, but these little things contribute in their own way to your growth.

6. **Get rid of gifts and memories** - Now might be the right time to take a step forward and physically remove all the carriers of your ex's memories. It is advisable to get rid of all the gifts that your ex might have given you. Even if you find it unnecessary or difficult to throw away the gifts, it is better if you do so. How can these gifts or memories serve you now? They are only painful reminders of the past. Get rid of them as soon as possible.

If you think that you have stuff that is too good to be thrown away, consider donating the stuff to the needy. A shirt or a toy can bring a smile on the face of somebody who desires them. Those smiles will make you happy. You should also throw any old photographs and letters that you might have. Delete the photographs that might be uploaded on the social media or stored in your computer. Think of this process as a way to make space for new photographs and memories of the life that is to be.

7. **Maintain your peace of mind** - Sometimes, even after all the efforts you do, something that is beyond the scope of your control can trigger your memory. For example, a certain dish might remind you of your ex lover or a certain scent might take you to old times. When you face such a situation that you have no control over, it is better to just face it and be done with it.

Look at the dish, take in the fragrance, acknowledge those memories and just move on. You don't have to linger around anything for too long, and you don't have to run away from anything. There is no harm is acknowledging good times, while trying to move on. Just keep your peace of mind and rest will follow.

8. **Why are you better without your ex?** - Make a list of all the things that you didn't like in your ex lover. This seems like a mean thing to do. But, it can be an important step in your way to progress. There could be certain things about your ex that irritated you even when you were in the relationship. There might be some habits that you hated. This list could also contain points on why the breakup is better for you. The list could consist of serious issues that you had or even the silliest things, such as he spoke too fast or too loud and he snored while sleeping. The aim of this list is not to put someone down and

31

yourself up, but only to help yourself. Go through this list whenever you feel like you are losing track.

This list would help you remember the things that you need to remember. Sometimes a person can fall into the trap of romanticizing the past. Avoid doing this because doing this will make you forget the real reasons for the breakup by focusing too much on the good times. The relationship might have had some good times, but those times are over. The relationship would have still been there if it was only about good things. There were issues that led to the breakup. Irrespective of who broke up, you or your ex lover, accept the issues that you guys had. Accepting these issues will not let you forget the real reasons for the breakup.

9. **Remind yourself of your life before your lover** - You should not

lose track of your own life when in a relationship with somebody else. But, more often than not people immerse themselves so much in a romantic relationship that they forget about their own personal likes and dislikes. Remind yourself of your life before your ex.

What did you like doing in your free time? What were your hobbies? Which places did you like visiting? What did you enjoy eating? These simple reminders will take you back to a time when you were surviving fine in the absence of your lover. If you could do it then, can't you do it now? Definitely, you can. It is not impossible, just a little complicated. But, once you are on the road to recovery, sooner or later you'll get there.

10. **Forget, forgive and let go** - You might have been wronged. The treatment given to you might be

extremely unfair. You might have a lot of hurt in your heart. But, this hurt and anger should not hamper your life in a negative way. No matter how strong your impulse might be to get hold of your ex to teach him a lesson, you should learn to let it go. Letting go will help you more than anybody else. You have to focus on forgiving and forgetting.

Forgiving does not mean that you are weak; instead it means that you have the grit and courage to accept your life's challenges without any malice in your heart. Even if you were at fault, forgive yourself. Don't commit the same mistakes in the future, but for now be kind to yourself and forgive yourself. Forgive the other person for his or her mistakes and forget about them. You have a life to focus on. You can't sit and focus on other's mistakes.

11. **Don't turn into a cynic** - Breakups do happen, but that does not mean that there is no love for you out there. Don't become too cynical about love and relationships. Keep an open outlook towards people and relationships. If you restrict your thinking, it'll affect your future relationship. So, for now keep your heart and mind open and free. Love will come when it has to. You just have to be in the right frame of mind when it comes to you. A cynical person views all the events of his life on the basis of that one bad incident. Take care not to do this. Be normal and accept the things as they are.

12. **Keep an outsider's view** - It is important that a person views the entire situation and the breakup incident as an outsider. There is a difference when you lament over something and when you see someone else lament over the same thing. Your understanding of the

situation would be completely different. When you suffer an injury, you might feel that you are unlucky and all bad happens to you, but when you see someone else suffering from the same injury, you understand that the pain is temporary and that the person will be fine. Therefore, it is important that you view the event of your breakup and the situations that led to it from a distance, as an outsider.

As an outsider you might be able to understand that it was not a big deal and it should not affect your life in the long run. It will also teach you to be a stronger and better person. Once you realize that you have overcome all the turmoil that the breakup brought along with it, you will find yourself free and empowered.

Conclusion

Everything seems impossible after a heart break. People dream of a life together and then they have to leave each other mid way and move ahead in separate directions. While some breakups are amicable, some people go through really difficult breakups. There are all sorts of breakups, but they all hurt a lot. There is no such thing as an easy breakup. There are bound to be mood swings and depressing phases. But, the fact is that life has to and should move on.

A break up should not be the most significant event in your life. You might have thought that the relationship is forever and that the lover is your soul mate. No matter how much invested you were at an emotional level in the relationship, you can always make a strong come back after a breakup. There could be many reasons for a breakup, but no matter how bad the relationship or the breakup was, you still deserve all the love in the world. You need to be kind to yourself while going through a breakup.

This may seem as a very daunting task, but with a little thoughtfulness and care, it'll be easier than it sounds. Love yourself and give yourself another chance. Once you resolve to heal yourself, nothing can stop you. By following some easy steps listed in the book, you would get back with double power. Even if it seems difficult, don't give up and keep trying.

Good luck!